Tashlikh
by Tikva Hecht

Ben Yehuda Press
Teaneck, New Jersey

Published by Ben Yehuda Press
122 Ayers Court #1B
Teaneck, NJ 07666

http://www.BenYehudaPress.com

To subscribe to our monthly book club and support independent Jewish publishing, visit https://www.patreon.com/BenYehudaPress

Jewish Poetry Project #32   **http://jpoetry.us**

Ben Yehuda Press books may be purchased at a discount by synagogues, book clubs, and other institutions buying in bulk. For information, please email markets@BenYehudaPress.com

ISBN13 978-1-953829-52-8 paper

24 25 26 / 10 9 8 7 6 5 4 3 2 1   20240905

for nae and the rabbi, of course

Contents

Tashlikh

Afterwards

you find the hours on your clothes

not the whole of the hours   but what rubs off undetected
alongside stray hairs and stains   and the breath too

of everyone who talked to you   and the breath too
of your ideas   some decent
and others plain   this morning

you watched seagulls circle and land
the skill of their freedom stark and grating

against your body   you let those birds
against your imagination

without thinking once you'd like to be them
without thinking once they did not know

they had come to give you   an image
of being adrift   and being adrift well
and without thinking once

about them afterwards   what stays on you
anyway stays   and by night

your palms are sand and wail of oceans
misplaced between threads

I: Falling Bodies

Apology in the form of Necessity

Still the roses open wider,
a week old or two weeks,

the last petals of their hopeful bodies

already the texture
of a souvenir

dry and industrial and

under the force of touch,
see, they are unmoving

or they crumble. See,

this decay, and still, how wide
like gaping monsters

they become

as if to say:
No, it is not like that—

between life and

death,
balance

is not the word you want.

Tashlikh

We would rub the bread left from the night
into crumbs   drop crumbs into our pockets

with our thumbs first we made the crumbs—

gently, gently, so the edges will separate
                                        —I am trying

after a ritual—

after a way to remember—

too rough, and
sweat will
dampen the
crusts

                              We would walk then to water,
                        drop crumbs there in place of our sins

                  Watch. Crumbs won't break but curve the water

                        like a finger lightly pressing skin

                                        —is it because,
                                              to the body,
                                        to have chosen
                                  and to be choiceless
                                        feel the same,
                                        a want comes
                                              alongside
                                        kneeling leaves
                                              to discard
                              something of myself
                                              as well?

I would think about the fish snacking on our sins,
wasn't it a kind harvest we left, and well-salted?

Their tiny mouths, only a pulse
to place the touch of hunger against grain
                              —I believed they were sins
the way I became accustomed
to dreams or jokes,

how I accepted
my senses

as if waiting for
something else.

Try to understand

there is nothing to explain. What could liken anything to sin
better than strangeness?

                    Walk home when it is over,
                    fingertips in textured pockets

                              shake, shake them out
                              or strays may catch
                              in the seams

We would rub the bread left from the night
into crumbs   drop crumbs into our pockets

with our thumbs first we made the crumbs—

gently, gently, so the edges will separate
                                        —I am trying

after a ritual—

after a way to remember—   **After:** I saw her afterwards. My father's mother.
                                    A compact thing on and under white linen.

too rough, and
sweat will   I glanced in after my father. She seemed made of
dampen the   a strange material. One I had not seen before or
crusts   ever touched.

                                            I almost asked: what is that?

                            We would walk then to water,
                        drop crumbs there in place of our sins

                    Watch. Crumbs won't break but curve the water

                        like a finger lightly pressing skin

Something: It was our habit in the hospital
as well. She was alive then.   —is it because,
                                                        to the body,
The day for example the doctor explained: to have chosen
should it come to it, it was our choice, but should it come   and to be choiceless
to it, it would be better — let her go; she was already old.   feel the same,
                                                        a want comes
He was the one who knew.   alongside
And afterwards, we looked in to see that she was warm.   kneeling leaves
                                                        to discard
Here too, my father looks, as if to count her pillows or   something of myself
fold a fallen towel.   as well?

Everything is fine—

I would think about the fish snacking on our sins,
wasn't it a kind harvest we left, and well-salted?

Their tiny mouths, only a pulse
to place the touch of hunger against grain
                                        —I believed they were sins

the way I became accustomed
to dreams or jokes,

how I accepted
my senses   **Nothing**: He thanks the funeral director. Thanks the wall.
                                                      Thanks me.

as if waiting for
something else.   She lies there and I want to ask: Is it true?
                                        Did she lie like this all night?

Try to understand   She lay there, a compact thing reflecting the care
                                        of a florescent light.

there is nothing to explain. What could liken anything to sin
better than strangeness?

                              Walk home when it is over,
                              fingertips in textured pockets

                                        shake, shake them out
                                        or strays may catch
                                        in the seams

    Strays: Fingertips ringed with crumbs. A fallen towel.
    I almost asked what is that? I almost asked how will it need?

Apology in the form of Dissent

I think how I lived then untamed and three-headed
painted with two brush strokes on a single-ply tissue.

Let's try another one:

I think how my emotions stunk
a concentrated pus urged from the edges

of a too tightly wound bandage.

You did not do this to me
You did this to me

You did not—

It is embarrassing to love.
No. But to the extent it is

embarrassing to imagine?

In the sense
it is decent to want

less, to know what to do
with your wanting. To love.

I think how I did not feel then

almost anything
and so hugely.

Transience

Something forgets us perfectly
– Leonard Cohen

near by bodies
plaits of disquietudes and gladness   walk

here language still means something
very little

one will eat soon   will drink will be grateful

the body's calls not dull but inevitable
uninteresting to the imagination   the leaves
stilled in forms of agony   pretty and interesting

being in or being out of a body
seems almost the same thing

the self and the body almost two things
the air's practiced hand almost able
to slip sheets of finely woven
yearning between them without a rustle   Remember

the solicitation of your body
baring and painful   the possibility of being
in the wrong body   this wrongness fibrous and
all of you   the body's brokerage of assumptions
and lusts   who doesn't
want to skin themselves alive
sometimes

where to drink, what to eat, genesis as prosaic
as a possum in the tone
of calm occurrences and something—

it was autumn then too
or a mirroring spring
the wind stripped of hydration
and bodies occluded
contracted in the cold like bodies

Dissent in the form of Lyric

I

A draft weans off my parted fingers,
it will become the wind one day
it has such ambition.

Between my shoulder blades, an ache
between my recanting thoughts, a plea:

if I could love you gently—
if I could be to you what I am to the air—

if my hands
could form your sanctuary—

II

I remember him leaning into the chair back
so I thought this will crack. It was fine.

I remember his arms as two felled trees
commanding to be used.

They must have been folded across him.
He must have felt afraid. He did not like
how unpredictable I was.

What do you do, I ask him,
when you fall short of being
who you want to be? When you
fall short of your own standard?

I am my standard.

III

I don't know how to live like this:
to concede to the beatbeating self
over the imaginable one,

to ask another strength of love
other than to imagine,

to want nothing not already ingested.

IV

Here, feed on me still

I will make of you the wind.

Psalm

I don't know what to do
with just rain
such sacred sweeping grace
an alternative to tangled beauty
I don't know

what more would I want
than to gather grain
when the season comes
turn it to bread, eat
if I could

wouldn't I want
to touch my god
if I could
find an alternative
to faith
I don't know

Still Life with Water

These days are rough,
un-rhyming and overly repentant;

why do they hardly hurt?

The cupped palms of the waves and the wind
collect each other, escape each other.

The water, strong, hoarse, and steady
gnaws at the wind—let me rest—

coming for the wind
the way the cornered come.

She stands in the way of the wind

cupping her palms over her mouth
to warm them with her breath.

Come for me waves, she thinks,
I will not move.

Tempt me, she thinks,
I will not move,

thinking, maybe they will tempt me,
maybe I will move.

Imprint

Commonality with other people carries with it all the meanings of the word common. It means belonging to a society, having a public role, being part of that which is universal (…) It also carries with it a feeling of smallness, of insignificance, a sense that one's own troubles are 'as a drop of rain in the sea.' The survivor who has achieved commonality with others can rest from her labors (…) Her recovery is accomplished; all that remains before her is her life.
— *Judith Herman,* Trauma and Recovery

I

Maggie built a house by the sea
    Maggie, what have you done?

How you look at the waves
    without being one

it puzzles me

II

One night she watches Maytime with her mother, an old black and white

film from 1937. It's one of those stories of bad timing and forbidden love,

very sad. Her mother cries all through it. *I don't know why,* her mother says,

I'm so sad, I loved it when I was little. She had seen it when it first came out,

her mother had taken her to see it.

You had your whole life ahead of you then.
Yes, that's it, thank you.

And again, afterwards: *thank you.*

III

Maggie, what do you make
    of the tide?

Of the air it endows
    and then—

what then?

IV

There were years, she tells us, she could not speak about it in group. Not because she couldn't speak about it. My father raped me. My father raped me. See, it is easy enough. But because when she did, some of the others speaking after her would start with an apology, embarrassed by the meagerness of their own stories. Sometimes, for their sakes, she'd say it was an uncle. And she, herself, even until recently, would stand in front of the mirror naked, searching her body for a scar. Rummaging, she calls it, for change to pay her mourners.

Later, when this topic is exhausted, someone mentions a good story they heard. A giant squid was found washed up on a beach not too far from our hotel. The area is well known for a legend about a sea-monster able to encircle whole boats in its arms. Now the fishermen think their grandfathers

Tikva Hecht

must have just come across one of these squid. She laughs at that with the
rest of us. But why, she asks, is it any less of a monster because it is real?

V

And those pebbles,
    Maggie, don't they look cross?

I think the seaweed breaks
    and breaks their hearts

and the seashells—
    were they always so thin?

VI

If you had known her then, this is what
you would have known:

A girl sitting

not quite at, but alongside a table.

A finger hazarding to turn a page.

Sometimes a friend stops, sits while they eat.

The book closing, instantly and without flourish.

It opens when the friend leaves. Also without a sigh.

Which the distraction. Which the thing.

If a crumb is left on her fingertip

she slides her thumb there until long after

it is just skin.

VII

Oh, I think I would drown
    in the air like a fish

if I lived by the sea

    but then I think of Maggie—

Psalm

I

I have wanted to tell you for a long time
of my   something calls me tonight
there in the cup   your hand
and the doorframe straight as descent   we have
never found a soil rich enough   we have
never allowed   wait, stop,   I have something
to tell you I wanted to tell you
: all my life I have only sought to be water or Bach
we have learnt the border of our exchange we
have learnt the weakness of our banding we
have disbanded   well, want to come over?
all my life   I have wanted
to be the v between your thumb
and index finger I am trying to tell you
I am unhappy   I am trying to tell you
I am happy

II

I cannot tell you how simple I am.
All night I watch through blinds
headlights turning. This is all that is
of interest to me: how they turn
to diamonds and are yellow
or red. I know one day I may or I may not
end my life. I don't think
of who drives the cars. I don't think
of how. Something tonight calls me
and it is my body which bears the strain.
The crease between my lips tastes of salt
and I think of the chickpeas I will have tomorrow,
and of the tomatoes you might bring me.

Psalm

        we walk our bodies
through a dusk unforgivable: beauty with its bearings in the inevitable
caught where patience and mania arrange desire disarray   and it hurts

to be one thing   beauty a sense of severing an arthritis of the
  heart

and what to do with this skin   an irritant
between us   speaking idioms
in a language formed only in the past tense and

I wait
as a watchman waits and

I smile   we walk our bodies
fine and capricious hunger and casual talk   where to drink what to eat

to sweet fermented dawn which comes as expected as loss
as excavation: the sky clearing itself uncovering itself as it is   the same
only smaller

the beauty the boredom of autumn
sickening: they decide where to eat: I smile

waiting as a watchman
as a watchman waits
even after

Tikva Hecht

The Way We Hold Each Other

Against the greyhound station they
compare tattoos, discuss the news—
the economy's in fast decay:
against the greyhound station they
trace unicorns where dust lights grey,
slant beer bottles to rainbow their booze
against the greyhound station; they
compare tattoos, discuss the news.

So they turn

the two young people
with the sandy hair and scraped knees
wondering if they were ever
as noticeable or as enviable
as the lights turning over the water
and if they could be enviable
without being noticed
and if the lights really mean
to mock them or only look
intimate because they have been
leaning over the boardwalk railing
and balancing on the boardwalk
railing and now are dizzy
and feeling just good enough
to look at something they don't
know and remember something
they'll never know
But you know
one of them says
it's more tiring on the legs
to stand straight
than to run very far
and the other one nods
but not because of knowing
and says I remember my mother
standing on a beach
and I was wishing then
I had not hurt her so much
and the other one said did you?
and the other one said maybe not
and the other one said I'm tired.
They were tired, very tired
so they went home
the smell of envy

Tikva Hecht

distant from them
so they could not wash
the smell of distance
from their faces
even after a week.

The Disposition of Cannibals

Suck out the marrow, you say,
but don't pray to it—the empty bone
and the shiver, that's the good stuff. You say
what's left after appetite has expired,
after hope has turned,
that's the good stuff. You say
the only wisdom you can
stomach: We are here.
Nothing else
to do but be. The truth is,

you faint in the awe of stillness,
in the awe of loneliness,
same as I do, same as I collect
despair in its tiniest form
of flickering breath, punch holes for it
in the top of a mason jar, so it may live
a few days dressing a nostalgic scene
because such is beauty—
all that is powerful
all that floors us. The truth is,

I still long
for the glimmer and sorrow
of an infinite heart, crafted
from the finest materials
of an enchanted world, unfettered
by cravings or the cold; I imagine
this longing as the tips of glass wings
skimming the warmest, fertile havens
of an unaffected earth,
mounds of dirt upended and still
pristine. But the truth is,

I ripped my mother
from the inside
to get a taste of this world
and got away with it
because I cried
out of hunger.

She Tells Me She Has Suicidal Thoughts

so many
so many

      so this was where her voice lay low
these past weeks, and now they imitate
the waves that rushed us, first time
at the ocean, jeans rolled to the thick of our calves
and still   it wasn't long before we wore
a sample of the ocean's body, clothes heavy as a child
swinging from our necks; sat then like happy things
who had never forsaken movement, and language
was a tonic of breath and salt and a pulse impatient
with life, brimming with life,
with only sound for what we knew
by heart, saying over and only
                so beautiful
                so beautifull

over and again
as if words could imitate the rush of waves,
carry us where they might

Acceptance in the form of Aside

The cold is wonderful this side of the glass
all things easy to praise.

I warm soup, pour a glass of wine,
another cup of tea   excess in wait of erasure—

well, isn't that what memory is?
And did you guess, at night

I dream we are happy. Isn't that strange?
Do you remember how it used to be?

I would shudder awake from a dream
that you were raping me

and you would want to calm me
and it scared you.

I have never dreamed, you said,
of someone I love hurting me.

I have never dreamed, you said,
of being afraid of my love.

We embraced a theory that dreams
are peopled entirely by the dreamer

taking the form of those they know.
It gave a little comfort to think it was only

in my image we warred.
We did not ask—why did we not ask—

why I took your form, or abstractly: why
the form of this one

over that? Or why at all?
How it scared you,

how your fear seeped from where
you stashed it, so much fear

I mistook it for your breath—like one might
mistake air for breath—

and did nothing
as it saturated the walls

and my skin and beneath
my skin.   How sweetly

last night we treated one another
in my image.

Have I learned then to love myself?
Ach, the wind,

it reeks of look-at-me
and tender hesitancy, still a combination

that tugs at my sentiments. Fine,
tug—on condition you stay outside. Stay

where you may be
useful to an image and I will be

where I have these words
and the wine, the tea, the soup,

these words, they pile, look
how they pile, eager as kindling,

to be consumed.

There are holes in our hearts

for the birds to fly through
ice cream trucks and freight trains
    play their blues

oh the holes in my heart
    where you went through
doo bee doo doobeedoo

bark dogs, bark your old age dues
    holes in your fur and one ear
where the cat got through
    but not you

with holes in your jeans
    for knees to get through—hands too

when was the last time
    a little avalanche swallowed
in you and sad fell through?

well isn't sad a hole too?
    it's almost night now
and old women won't say
    what they've been through

so what can you do?
    oh these holes in my heart
wings tickle and itch
    when the birds fly through.

Apology

The birds of the end of summer tap their beaks
against each other's necks. Do no harm. Seem
to rustle the water as they rustle the empty sky—
not because one touches the other, but because nothing
lies between. The birds of the end of summer
slide their beaks behind each other's necks. Do not kiss.
Weigh on extended wings the temperature or the time.
Not too concerned.
      This is a season of unconcern
as if we owned it always and may not
want it forever. It sits heavy outside the chest,
murmuring under and over the breath, patient
as the swans or the preening sun:
if you wait, by winter you will be numb.

Well, isn't this true, birds?
Though which of us believes in winter.

Les Noces

after William Carlos Williams

If I when my job is over
and the last love and the love before that
are over
and the air is a steel kiss
between fraying curtains
and staccato trees—
if I in my cotton leggings
and oversized sweatshirt
dance decadently
avoiding the mirror
off-beat and no song
slapping my empty womb—

who shall say that I am not
the street sweeping mystic
of my own kingdom?

II: Configurations of Worship

Construction

Alas, for with better thoughts
I would have been able to create holy angels
—Rabbi Avraham Danzig, Tefilla Zaka

Seems juvenile, I know, to lay between minds and metaphysics
such open borders, egotistical too, as if to think is just the same
as to cup a sparrow, and whoosh—open palm—watch it forget you.

But what can I do? My clumsy thoughts suffer
from a stubborn will.

Just don't ask me, I tell them, which of you are best suited.
You will have to see after your own holiness,

or ask the angel
when he is ready—*he?*

Perhaps not.

Who can tell among all these feathers, prolific as popcorn,
hiccupping into existence. Really, you have never felt such wings!
Heavy as a drunken fur coat. Here, you could sink a whole hand

and find coins, the skin of a desert snake, a deflated balloon, two
feathers of a different color, some folded hopes
to be delivered later, a few crumpled tissues.

But that has nothing to do with my mind—

No, that is just my angel.

Tikva Hecht

She opened a shop

                             a corner store
where she sells beliefs   she sold before
vacuums door to door   so she knows the business
but she wanted more   her own place
to stay put   her own shelves
to keep clean   and Lord, how she dusts
nimbly between   ribbons and tissue paper
along the counter top   (in case you might ask
for gift wrap)   you can browse
if you like; she doesn't care   if you touch her ware
she's touched it herself   it's durable she swears
though some's better for wear   and once in a while
she's just out of stock   still, she has an eye
for the right size   and a sense of décor
plus reinforcements galore   words and ointments
that will keep you coming back   some say she reads minds
some say she's just smart   three kittens in the back room
come and go as they please   her hands catch their ears
what to do what to do with herself   after-hours and there's
nothing she wants   she locks the door
checks the lock   once twice once more
she wants to make sure   she'll hear if it rattles
she waits to hear   the crash of glass
the thud of a thief   piling her beliefs
into a sack—oh, wouldn't   some intrusion
help pass the night   and besides
she's always supposed   what a thief
would take   has got to be right

Configurations of Worship

I

The poet sips her water; carries on.
Of course, in my work, God is always a metaphor.

A student interrupts.
For what?

What?

A metaphor for what?

The poet leans forward
as if to spit.
For God, of course. What else?

The student does not know. The poet carries on.

II

I am an anatomy of false gods and if you ask how anyone can be so stupid,
    I will ask back—what worship isn't the worship of what can be made
    from dust and from flames, from muscling thoughts and long pleas? I
    will tell you every conception of god is a false god made in the image of
    god. Which is to say every conception of god is a conception of self. And
    every self the mirage of god posing as a false god and so—you do the
    math. I am tired of this logic and its aesthetic. Please god, let me be rid
    of you.

III

The student explains to his cat that what makes a poem good is its
    necessity.

It must rid silence of what needs to be said.

The student explains to his poem that it is saying too much.

What makes a poem good is how closely it mouths what cannot be said.

The student explains to the poet that he could not complete the
    assignment.

I'm not any good.

IV

I have tried to be good. That is a lie.
I have tried. I have tried.

Go on.

V

The poet had asked the students
to write a prayer.

The poet had asked the students to name the prayer
after themselves.

The poet likes names.
The poet likes the idea of names.
They remind us of what is not
interchangeable.

The poet does not like her name.
The poet does not like the idea of her name
incorporated. *It seems a kind of embalmment.*

No, just a way to save on taxes,

says her accountant.
The poet likes this accountant.
This accountant's name is Stu.
The poet likes this name.
It reminds her of nothing.

VI

I don't think I can write until I've read more. I've never read Hamlet.

Shakespeare never read Hamlet either, until he wrote it.

Is that a metaphor?

Go write a poem.

A metaphor for God?

Monday, your poem on my desk.

VII

I want to touch the damp earth and become of it. I want to weep an
    indecipherable language. I want with precise kisses for you to taste this
    language and speak of it. I want to bind our longing into sheaves and call
    it prayer and call it poetry and call god to give testimony on our behalves
    and together half listen.

VIII

The poet thinks of Stu.
The poet thinks of Stu
even when nothing reminds her of him.
The poet thinks of Stu
because nothing reminds her of him.
He is like nothing, the poet thinks.
The poet likes this. It seems
pure. But the poet would not use this word.

Stu has a partner.
Stu has three children.
Stu likes poetry.
Stu remembers liking poetry. In school.

IX

On Tuesday the student leaves his poem on the poet's desk.
The poem is a blank sheet of paper; blank, that is, except for the title:
Go Figure

X

Me and god, we're like two discarded skins, each mistaking the other for a
    body.
My body and me, we're like two discarded gods, each mistaking the other
    for a name.

XI

I liked your poem.

Did you get it?

I don't need to get it. I liked it.

But did you get it?

I don't think you understand how poetry works.

It's a metaphor.

For what?

You didn't get it?

I need to fail you. I said Monday.

But you liked it?

Yes. It's a terrible poem. But I liked it.

Good. I don't care if I fail.

XII

I have tried to care for your wisdom. I don't
know what good it has done. I have tried to care
for your creations. I don't know
if I do. I have tried to create.

Go on.

Isn't that enough?

XIII

The poet shows Stu the student's poem.
He laughs, he likes it.
The poet asks him if he gets it.
He doesn't think there's anything to get.
The poet folds the page and puts it away.

Don't let him get away with that,
he'll start thinking everything's profound.

I really shouldn't share student work.

Does it matter? I don't know his name.

His name is his work.

XIV

Did you mean to leave us your delicate peels, spiral figures on a tile floor, a
    film of sweet flesh barely left by the knife to line each curl? Traces rich
    with what they are not; the fruit grows in the air. Did you mean to leave
    us your likeness in yearning? Prints of it line the kitchen drawers, lie
    tucked below uneven table legs, wrap like fat around thighs around and
    around and around. I have a name for you my mouth does not know. It
    is like four fingers resting on the down of an arm they do not touch.

No, it is not *like* that at all.

I Came to the Edge of the World

Edge, I said, what is below you?

No, the edge said, that is not the question.

Edge, I said, what is beside you?

No, the edge said, that is not the question.

Edge, I said, what is above you?

Stupid, the edge said, see for yourself.

Edge, I said, don't you love me?

Edge, I said, don't you know me?

Edge, I said, what is the question?

But the edge had gone away.

The Angel Made of My Thoughts Sings of the Man with Paper
  Wings

I

The man with paper wings,
oh, the man with paper wings
knows so manymany
interesting things.

He knows where moths gather
under melancholic light
and what exactly are the differences
between eighty-six varieties

of flight.

II

He calls the moths iridescent. Their flight
is his favorite. He calls it just short
of stillness.

Elation, he says, *must be like that.*
But I don't know
if he is asking or commanding.

Once, I tell him, *I landed squarely*
on a just-opened oven door.
And later? he asks me.

It hurt.
And just before?
I wanted to see someone in a different room.

He wants to believe I am the memory
of that someone in the different room.
I want to believe in the morning

the grass will be
the color of these moths
and will chime.

Nobody gets everything they want.

As the sky darkens, as movement
darkens, as the eye splits,

I scrape his measure into mine.
You know, there are days I do not like to fly.

I say this to make him happy. It doesn't.

I would recognize myself anywhere,
he says, *by the back of my absence.*

Halfway Down

Lines in italics make up the full poem "Halfway Down" by A. A. Milne.

Halfway down the stairs
    ash in white dresses
Is a stair / Where I sit.
    that's what she says we are
There isn't any / Other stair
    but who, she adds, isn't
Quite like / It.

so we smile at the officers
    I'm not at the bottom,
who smile at us
    I'm not at the top;
and smile at the stumbling man
    So this is the stair
who calls us kikes and cunts
    Where / I always / Stop.

she says how well
    Halfway up the stairs
can the body remember
    Isn't up, / And isn't down.
she says innocence scars
    It isn't in the nursery,
like habits and scars
    It isn't in the town.

And all sorts of funny thoughts
    who burnt us? / who dressed us?
Run round my head:
    she asks then quickly adds
It isn't really / Anywhere
    well, history is interesting
It's somewhere else
    what else is it?
Instead

Nijinsky / Nijinska

Lines in italics come from the diary of Bronislava Nijinska, except for the
last two, which are from the diary of her brother, Vaslav Nijinsky.

It was around when
     her brother was going mad
she heard he was dancing
     in London or dead.
Each stranger she asked after him
     until he was mad.
She lay on her own bed
     sick of heart or near dead.
Her children hungry, her husband
     gone, her students
sat by her bed as she shed
     delirium and filled notebooks—
something flickering in my
     ill brain ... my students
are starting to walk—it was
     a grade school notebook,
the same her brother used,
     though only once
he mentioned her,
     how he pretended to be mad
so she would stay away. As for her,
     she wrote of him: that once
times were better her dancers
     would dance for him (his being mad
a bully at her will) but
     mostly she wrote
of her own inventions,
     abstractions and ugliness
swelling beauty, the torture
     of movement through rote
technique and the nights
     she danced with the ugliness

     Tikva Hecht

away for a while,
       giving them [her
audience] *a sense of a different life.*
       It kept her alive
I have been told that
       I am mad. They say now about her—
strange, brilliant, ill-tempered woman   *I thought that*
       I was alive.

On Misplacement

Have they vanished forever, both Heaven and Hell?(…)
Let us implore that it be returned to us,
That second space.
– Czeslaw Milosz

You ask for heaven back. I search
around my feet. Turn out my pockets.
How long, I wonder, has it been miss-
ing and wouldn't I have noticed?

Once we tied a helium balloon, its light
blue skin stretched brutally with flight,
to the birdbath in our backyard and
did not notice when it was gone, only
that the sun for a while speared the lit-
tle pool at the tip of a curved shadow,
and then that this stopped and the sun
dozed soft and even across the bare
water.

Remember, months later, we found
the busted thing frozen to a branch?
You said the knot must have loosened
while we were not looking, but maybe
it was while we were looking, looking
right at the thing bob in and break-in
the wind, but had mistaken it for sky.

You: know who you are; often earnest, even asking after a bit of cloud to dress the gate posts.

You ask for heaven back. I search around my feet. Turn out my pockets. How long, I wonder, has it been missing and wouldn't I have noticed?

Heaven: the stillness —what stillness! count it! how will you count it?— that comes tucked between delight and disappointment in transience, in what waits, sweet as buoys, to be upturned.

For heaven: well, what else could explain how we exhibit, between the warring strains of what will be and what has been, such a tolerance for play, as in infants, struggling to play.

Once we tied a helium balloon, its light blue skin stretched brutally with flight, to the birdbath in our backyard and did not notice when it was gone, only that the sun for a while speared the little pool at the tip of a curved shadow, and then that this stopped and the sun dozed soft and even across the bare water.

Remember, months later, we found the busted thing frozen to a branch? You said the knot must have loosened while we were not looking, but maybe it was while we were looking, looking right at the thing bob in and break-in the wind, but had mistaken it for sky.

Ask for heaven:
what must wait what cannot wait.

Back:
ach! look what you've done   don't you know heavens grow like mushrooms
without mothers   just the word is fertile   come listen
it plays in me now   come don't you hear

rendition after rendition of amended hours   what else
is a heaven made of?   what else but a heaven

and a halved worm
insist so stubbornly on themselves?   what a strain! and still

what can you do?

how ruthlessly hope balks
how incessantly other worlds are made   out of this one.

Tashlikh   53

Holding

They leave their cigarette ends
in the worn down spaces between bricks

as if all they want is held there
written in tiny script

deep inside those butts
for God to uncurl and read.

I see it this way because of the Western Wall
where the mortar is amended by folded notes of prayers,

as if the stones can hold their posture for so long
only because the words know where the stone trembles,

and balance there, slight as children, holding steady the weight,
acting as the sages thought to make their words do,

hoping to hold a fallen temple
with study and prayer.

You say you will take me to this country
the one with this old wall, groped between caresses

by the faithful and the traditional and the doubting
as if to touch it right would release a tangible euphoria

from the next world into this,
this country where the wilted ground in the dry breeze

is unusually beautiful in its barrenness the way
death prays for life, until it is remembered,

where in the streets you see over shoulders

guns as large as the ones I used

to water my brothers and our friends,
friends who went to this country

high and without finishing high school,
to come back decent, wearing black suits and black hats,

to marry young, have babies, talk about going back.
The ones who, my mother reports, still smile well

and blink the rest back. Fine.
Take me to this country, show it to me

the way it is for you, the way you fit
your desire and its expression

where the build-up of history
should make space obsolete

if not for the way history decays too
into sentiment, so you are sure you will fit

or it will fall without you,
where if you took me

we would leave our cigarette ends
resting on the sand lining Tel Aviv

or in the cracks of that dry breeze
so they touch nothing of the land,

look nothing like the waiting prayers
they may be.

Félix Fernández García

in memory / in erasure

I can't remember myself
if I danced on the steps
of St. Martin-in-the-fields
or lay on the altar nude.
I certainly don't remember
removing my necktie
         and if the rumors
of my death are true, I can't say
but I have wound a wreath
from the straw at my feet is it true
they dance the same steps every night?

         In London's rain I carried your metronome
                  marking my grave
         barren walk but it became the rain
                  here it rains
         rising from the ground
         through the twitch of my sole
                  ah well,

I leave you the arch of my back
I leave you the pride of my instep
I leave you your promise. My turns
already have your company and,
   if you will,
bar history from my wake
who stepped between me and my makers,
and water my grave with silk.

Félix Fernández García: a flamenco dancer, (18?-19?)
discovered by the Ballets Russes, 1917

I can't remember myself
if I danced on the steps
of St. Martin-in-the-fields
or lay on the altar nude.
I certainly don't remember
removing my necktie
    and if the rumors
of my death are true, I can't say
but I have wound a wreath
from the straw at my feet is it true
they dance the same steps every night?

if I danced: while living
in London, where
he moved
for the Ballets Russes;
and where, we know,
he did something
that landed him
in an asylum

if the rumors: of Garcia's death, circa 1920s

a wreath: like the one
the Ballets Russes
might have hung
as they mourned Garcia,
as they would
any one
of their own

In London's rain I carried your metronome
    marking my grave
barren walk but it became the rain
    here it rains
rising from the ground
    through the twitch of my sole
      ah well,

they dance the same steps: as was the practice of the choreographed Ballets Russes, as was not the practice in flamenco

your metronome: as rumored,
Garcia walked
with a metronome
to exorcize his impulse
to improvise

twitch of my sole: it did not work

I leave you the arch of my back
I leave you the pride of my instep
I leave you your promise. My turns
already have your company and,
    if you will,
bar history from my wake
who stepped between me and my makers,
and water my grave with silk.

your promise: a leading role in exchange for teaching the company flamenco, a tradition never before taught outside its own world

your company: choreographed by
Massine,
who danced the part
in the end
who, as rumored,
always wanted the part
for himself
anyway

history: isn't that what you call an inside joke explained to strangers?

water my grave: but not until the 1940s, when Garcia, in fact, actually died, still in the asylum

On My Grandparents, Men Who Died Young of Incurable Diseases and Women Who Grew Very Old Without Their Memories

I

It sounds bad but it's not unusual and in the meantime

hurried air leaves on my window sill
a harvest offering tithed from mechanical devices
and conversation   *of them*   *what then*
                    come then   *come see*

these shards of sounds, they trample me, leave
nothing unmarked, roll my imagination painless
                    and then   *stop*
                            one second   *please*

and flat
            please—

until all sense of myself becomes something immediate
                    wait   *no*   *wait please*

and something haphazardly analogous to that immediacy
                    please see

as if such scattering is all that ever happens between wills
                    now what gets
                            please

and there has never been   *come then*
                    come see

more to me than them, or more to them than this breeze.

II

the afternoon jumps
      so does the heat

don't bother me, I ask. Please—

      I was told, talk about the rain
what do I know to say

      I cannot even talk
about the heart

      I keep remembering
the strong personality death had

      how he twisted afternoons
I stood and watched

      what a personality death had
he gave the hours fever

      but I have nothing to say now even to him
and he has grown bored of me

      between us now there is nothing

the afternoon scratches
      at me it scratches. Please, I ask.

I am waiting for something quiet
      I keep forgetting such a quiet thing

could have known such a bellow as death.
      I remember then something else

not memory—as memory has become
     a scrawl in the corner of my

expressions—but the sense I wait
     for what already is

like a kettle, left on and whistling

The Angel Made of My Thoughts Writes a Good-bye Note Then Boards the Wrong Train

When it is like this, this world
perfectly laid flatware
self-content in its thisness,
pain slips away from every surface.

I'm sorry,
I do not know now
where your pain is.

I go look for it in Brooklyn.

I think, my little creator,
how this would disappoint you.
You wanted me more proficient.
You wanted that I should use
the salt from your tears
to preserve the meat
of your mid-day offerings.

I am not so proficient.
I only look efficient
because I am alone
in Flatbush with old people in a park.

This one gossips with that one's tremors.
These play a game of chess they just played.
And those, who sit quiet as justice? Yes,
they too teach assertion, if only
in the form of indifference.

I think how this is like you.
How it might be like you
but I don't remember

whose move it was, who touched and who
was touched. When I make my way home
the day leans like a teenager against the train window.

What? You think I say this to explain?
I am not the day. I am not
the melody it plays between this
and this and if I put lyrics to it?
What could that explain?

And if still later I hum?

Theology

So you say, burn your temples
and I will burn mine

but dutiful is the rain
and nothing will catch.

There is no lack of imagery
on this softening earth,
no bar on the imagination,
no escape from conjecture, nothing
that cannot be believed in, and still,
you recoil from belief
as from a meaningless, distasteful joke.

Please you think to ask
return to me my past
and in exchange—

there is always an exchange—

please you think to ask
allow me to stop with this belief.

You think you will find something calmer
something cool and elegant in the storehouse
of acceptance,

you think you will be less ashamed.

Come, learn first the name of one thing
and then you can try out this thinking.

Come, learn first the body of one name
and then you can try out this god.

The Angel Made of My Thoughts Dusts the Ceiling of the Sistine Chapel Then Sells Me the Dirt Off Her Feathers

I want to say to you
sometimes,
     I know why
you call it courage

to be so afraid

Knob

When the door opened
when the door swung
when the door creaked
when the door
opened
you were standing there
and I did not care.
I've always liked doors.

I broke my tooth
my toe
my nose
my aunt's vase
against doors.

I've closed them on fingers
and at the wrong time and at the right time
and leant against them for the drama
and scratched
my fingers, and banged
my fingers, and pressed
my fingers against
so many doors. My favorite

the big wooden ones or glass
ones that slide and hide
Nothing. I'd make
a world full of doors where
I could always arrive and never
get in. I'd like it that way

I'd just open doors and close
doors, listen to them bang
or be knocked.

While Looking at the Portrait of Patience Escalier Between Mincha and Ne'ila

May it be Your will (...) that I shall sin no more,
and the sins I have committed before You, erase them (...)
but not through suffering and severe illness
—from the Yom Kippur liturgy

I

The hand
yes I have been that hand
the one quieted under the other
and the other
I have been it too
have brushed wide palmed,
fingers thick and bent like old bristles,
the untanned brow
beneath that hat   I have been the hat

And you?
the kerchief perhaps
the color of dried blood
the collar unnaturally creased
the eyes
are his eyes
but the accessories
they are ours   aren't they
isn't this why we stare as if
inventing sight
not to become someone else
but because here we are close to being
all things
other than an old man
with a curious look

what a curious look
he has   as if he does not
understand why anyone
has asked him
to keep still and still
as if he is grateful
to be of use to someone
in his stillness and still
kind enough not to say
to the man who needs him
that what he has to give
can not be what is needed
because what is needed
does not settle
into colors and lines   is not
the look or the stillness
but the work

it is then when belief spreads easily
suggests when the mood settles
we may stay like this still
his look against mine   a prayer

comes then
for all the work
the suffering and illness
of redemption   yes
come   I will work   only

spare me

a suffering an illness too severe   for me

I am not his hand I am not even its rest
and I have only picked at devotion
as the artist must have stopped

to pick stray bristles from the end of an old paintbrush
or a child might pick at the edges
of a straw hat such as his
discarding strands like half-remembered lyrics
not expecting the residue piling there to become
everything left of the thing itself.

II

—oh

       Patience

      a joke perhaps
against the pleading in his seeping face

                      To that face

its angles worshipped by colour
          into constellations
I bow down

as I bow to the persistent hoarders of faith
fingernails dirty with devotion

as I bow to you   to the days you walk
until the arrival of one new thought
to the hours you hold your hands against
their strength until they shake
to the kindness that runs the length of your
refusal   to the goodness
that runs the length of your salted words
to your repentance

How softly the old man stares   softly

he knows   his is breath that can melt the paints
of the master   and then?   Not us not one of us
could be still any longer

                         To the elementary
condition of waiting and its tender exhale—

Oh, the old man and his striped shirt

The Angel Made of My Thoughts Uses Her One Phone Call

All this talk

it keeps us, I know, from becoming
each other when our bodies are not looking,

only, I do not believe
tongues should be used like hands.   The old sages agreed,
                                   said that words,

                    such as 'here, this is yours'
                    or 'here, take this from me'

                    were *only* words, effecting
                    no exchange until an object was

                    lifted, tugged, used; unless,
                    of course, you were giving

                    something to God, in which case
                    words *only* words do anything,

                    action seeming, perhaps,
                    disrespectful in this case, given,

                    God used words,
                    only words they say

                    to make all this, but then
                    is it even words we mean,

                    or inclinations? And what can those
                    ever effect? Well, sin, of course,

                    and angels I have read. But
                    between two bodies,

what can one thought give
to an other?

Enough,
I tell you,

my tongue hurts from all this
in a different language

than my longing first spoke,
I didn't even know

half as well until I said it:
how misplaceable it is—

what we imagine
we want—

no better than keys.

III: Songs of Creation and Its Infidelities

Lines in italics are from the Rosh Hashanah liturgy, the Yom Kippur liturgy, Psalm 114, Moses Maimonides' *The Guide for the Perplexed*, *The Craft of Research*, 2nd Edition, and an interview with Eugène Ionesco. See the notes at the end of this book for specific attributions.

If my dreams are good, strengthen them
and if they require curing, cure them

      though you insist I could be otherwise
      as simply as you are others'

I am yours
and my dreams are yours

           [Dreams are reality at its most profound...
              invention, by its nature, can't be a lie.]

      Tikva Hecht

I have one, a dream

that we could live

kneading this life

what we know of it
what we do not know

cautiously and

that through
floured fingers we could

some of it hardens in our hair

crusts on our eyelashes

six times I called your name   and you didn't answer

He interrupts me.
He wants to know
Where the bottle opener is.

I make out of wine
And his lips metaphors
Because I cannot say

No, I do not know.

We both would rather not speak this night.
I find him the corkscrew.
He keeps me around.

here, I have another:

that you look on the sky's complexion
until it is your own

what there is to love rough with hesitation

that this time you interrupt—
   so the moon is whole
   well then
   we're allowed to be mad—

that you look
until it is my own

what there is to love as irrefutable as an illusion

six days I came to your name   and it turned to plaster

[*Some fail to acknowledge*
Alternatives, because they can't think
Of anything to acknowledge

Others can think
But fear if they acknowledge
They weaken their argument

A third
Can imagine objections
But lack the vocabulary]

this one too:

that between us the quiet startles
a flock of words

that we are these words
which pilfer the air

that we are this air

that we share our breath
each in a womb of the other

and upon falling back asleep:

that you part the tattered light
gathering satisfaction as it burrs on your fingers
bristled and healthy
                    to put into my hair

six plasters I made of your name   and they turned to dust

Our predicament goes well with warmed silence.

He, preoccupied by shards of himself
Angled once by him into me; me, my madness ensuing
Entreats him.

How well the idea of him stays put
Where I am cavernous

Just as he stays put
In other women.

and once:

of a room where we live

of life, the suds on the floor
   after baths

six worlds I made of your dust   they fill the space between my
   floorboards

The difference between us
I finally tell him:

I offer words

As they offer me:
Alms of desire and invention.

He invents.

His words rising
As Titans and ending

As algorithms.

I dream a dream
And do not know its meaning.

He does not dream.

and once:

of a prayer which soldiers through your throat
but fools your lips like water

that this water
shields more forms of loneliness
than sounds
and that some
          are pleasant

very pleasant

six tribes I sent to gather your name   but they only scattered

He is like a dream   when I wake.
As stranded as a dream

When I wake
I walk the dark halls to his notebooks.

If my dreams are good, strengthen them

He has plenty of notebooks.
They keep the past
Reserved for alterations.

Doesn't he know so many ifs
Dissect a reader.

This is why I flinch
When I find him behind me.

Not because he is behind me
And does not say since when.

and more than once:

that you die and tell me afterwards

if they ask for affection
            offer them coffee

that you sing from your grave—

slip a touch to earth
but keep to yourself enough

to pay the ransom of your birth

six curses I sent in pain over your name   they only flattered

See him walk to the other side of the room.

Well, what I liked first about him was watching him walk.

An always-away walk. In it he shelters his indiscretions and elegance
                    With one of a number of handmade necessities:
                    Providence, retribution, repentance, requital.

                              He wants me to know
                         What I want. What I expected.
                              What now I expect.
                              And what I will give
                                   To get it.

What I liked second about him was watching him walk.

              A gait conceived of sacrifice to atone, to make atonal
                    What is wrong   What is right.
: *True reality*
is illustrated
by sacrifice
the offering of sacrifice
a great and manifest
utility

                              As long as there is sacrifice
                         The past does not have to stay
                                   Wrong or right.

                                   But me?

                         I still dream that dream.
                    The mountains skipped like lambs
                    The hills like young lambs.

and this one, too:

that in your arms I become the wall

smiling like stale, dissipating sin
and chipped plaster

that in an unfamiliar front hall
we stand between parallel mirrors

the image of your face   everything

your face
          only reflection

an imitation of wisdom
effaced and infuriating

and a delight

six pollsters I sent to detain your name   they chatted

What he liked first about me?

He liked when I showed him my notebooks.

How I held them
As if water pooling in my hands
Afraid to wake their words.

I show him my notebooks now.
Two to a fist. Four. Six.

Here. Here see.

: Since you have no use for what I know of devotion
Won't you take this ash from my fantasies
To spice with the salt of your palm?

Drink. Drink to your health.

He watches the pages tear as I turn,
Fall with their overtones to the floor.

: No cause will ever be found
that one particular sacrifice
consists in a lamb
another in a ram
or that the victims
should be one particular number

and once:

that we are a study
of the collapse of sliding rain
blending our reflections into company

tell me, *what is with the mountains*
that they skip like lambs (not rams)
the hills like young lambs?

six lovers I sent to strain your name
but they only mattered   to the floorboards

And then?

        We went back to bed.

              I caught him stealing remnants of my loneliness
       While I slept. Jealous, I guess.
                    Of my longing   what else?
                    Of my madness

                           what else?

: All those who occupy themselves
with finding are stricken with madness

                         Ah, yes.

                         I try
                         I try
                      Still I

     I dream a dream in the dim mid-afternoon
            And do not know its meaning.

Tikva Hecht

of your limbs
left with the ache of playfulness
a quiet assurance gracing them
          a quiet cooling sweat

and then:

of sleep

six floorboards arranging a tune for your name   what a noise

And now?

See, this clumsy binding
Glue stains and a cardboard spine.

The point being: I keep my notebooks too.

And he

He keeps to himself.

I do not know if this is wrong or right.
It is not very sweet and many times I miss the bitterness of his touch.

and once:

of the small corners of your body
        of god

which the metaphor which the lust

one noise had I made   before you slipped from your name—oh
        it would've had you running

And that on occasion I practice how to say
As though it were just another thing to:

What a strange, I had such a strange—

Tikva Hecht

that you

that me

like a dog to the butcher's boots

Tikva Hecht

Notes

The use of glosses in *Tashlikh, On Misplacement,* and *Félix Fernández García* is inspired by the traditional page layout of the Babylonian Talmud.

Tashlikh is a ritual performed on Rosh Hashanah, the Jewish new year. Crumbs are thrown into a body of water to symbolize the desire to discard sins as easily.

"Something forgets us perfectly" comes from Leonard Cohen's poem *For E.J.P.*

Les Noces is inspired by William Carlos Williams' poem *Danse Russe.*

On Misplacement is a response to Czeslaw Milosz's poem *Second Space.*

Songs of Creation and Its Infidelities:

"If my dreams are good, strengthen them and if they require curing, cure them" and "I am yours and my dreams are yours" are from a prayer recited by the congregation during the Priestly Blessing on Rosh Hashanah.

"Dreams are reality at its most profound…" is from an interview with Eugène Ionesco, found in the book *Playwrights at Work.*

"Some fail to acknowledge…" is from *The Craft of Research, 2nd Edition,* by Wayne C. Booth, Gregory G. Colomb, and Joseph M. Williams.

"I dream a dream and do not know its meaning" is from the above-mentioned prayer recited on Rosh Hashanah.

"He is like a dream" is from the Yom Kippur liturgy. The full line from the prayer is "He is like a dream when he awakes".

"True reality is illustrated by sacrifice, the offering of sacrifice a great and manifest utility" is from *The Guide for the Perplexed*, by Moses Maimonides, translated by Shimon Pines.

"The mountains skipped like lambs, the hills like young lambs" is from Psalm 114.

"No cause will ever be found that one particular sacrifice consists in a lamb another in a ram or that the victims should be one particular number" is from *The Guide for the Perplexed*.

"What is with the mountains..." is from Psalm 114.

"All those who occupy themselves with finding are stricken with madness" is from *The Guide for the Perplexed*.

Acknowledgments

There are far more people than I can name here whose friendship, guidance or care have nourished me and by extension this book. I am grateful to all of you and hope that I will have the chance to thank you each personally. For now, and at risk of leaving someone out, I would like to thank just a few people to whom I am especially indebted for their direct involvement in and support of my writing and this book:

The editors of the following journals who published poems from this collection, sometimes in different forms: *Grain Magazine* ("Apology in the form of Necessity"); *Canadian Literature* ("Knob"); *The Lehrhaus* ("Configurations of Worship"); *The Jewish Literary Journal* ("Construction" and "Holding"); and *Untethered Magazine* ("She Tells Me She Had Suicidal Thoughts");

Larry Yudelson, editorial director at Ben Yehuda Press, and my editor at Ben Yehuda, Julia Knobloch, for their investment, patience and good humor throughout the editorial process, and for all the poetry they have helped usher into the world;

Joy Ladin for her early and continuing encouragement of me as an artist and as a human being — speaking to you always comes with the rare double gift of feeling seen and feeling galvanized to see;

Katie Ford, Allison Benis White and Erith Jaffe-Berg for their generous, astute and remarkably present mentorship during my time at UC Riverside, as well as the other faculty members and students at UCR who carefully read and responded to my work, in particular, Ilya Kaminsky and Emily Dorff;

Yavni Bar-Yam for reading multiple drafts of this manuscript, as well as every other piece of writing I send him, with unflinching care and tender honesty;

Jessie, who also read and commented on multiple drafts, for gripping with both hands where a poem turns into an encounter and for directing me towards the authentic;

Perel Hecht, Devora Levin and Emilia Cataldo for their feedback on all or some of these poems, for commiserating with me on all the weirdness and woes that come along with trying to make anything and for reminding me with their own art why it's worth it;

Sharon and Wayne Lacks and Chashi Skobac for reading all or some of these poems and for reading many more of my poems, all the way back to when I first started writing them;

Rabbi David Fohrman, Imu Shalev and Adina Blaustein for all the ways they have made me a better writer (who knew, sometimes clarity is a good thing), and Imu and Adina for their help brainstorming ways to promote this book;

and David Waldman for giving generously of his time and craft and wandering into the woods with me to take my author photo.

A few of the poems in this collection carry dedications:

Some years ago, I worked for a small non-profit providing preventative training on child sexual abuse in ultra-Orthodox Jewish communities. "Imprint" is for the survivors who shared their stories with me during that time and for Janie Perlstein, my colleague at the organization.

"On My Grandparents…" is in memory of my grandparents, Harry & Jennie Hecht and Rabbi Shraga Phyvle & Gitel Rosensweig, for my memories of their immersive affection, and for my aunt Chavi in memory of her David.

"Afterwards" is for Chaya Sarah Soloveichik and her steadfast friendship.

"The Way We Hold Each Other" is for Nathaniel Aharon and his kind, kind heart.

"So they turn" is for Dov Alpert and his indomitable imagination.

"On Misplacement" is for Reya, Chavatzelet, Shimshon, Amichai, Menucha, Nano and Binyamin Ori. You are my heavens. I hope you always find yours.

"While Looking at the Portrait of Patience Escalier…" is for my siblings — Razi the angel, Chai the seer and Dodi-lee our leader. It is hard enough to keep an honest eye on the world, hard enough to meet what-is with what-can-be and find the joke in it too, hard enough to be good — each of you do all three. Thank you for that, for all the ways you challenge me, for the mayhem and for each minute.

This book as a whole is for my parents — my father who taught me to learn as if my thoughts were creating the world, to think as if I were a guest in a world I did not create, to question with diligence, to serve with dignity, to see the big picture and to laugh to the edge of life. And my mother who edited every line, who taught me to write and before that to listen, and beneath that to live with one hand around beauty and the other reaching achingly and alive beyond this world, and somehow, hands full, to dance opened-palmed in the brilliant rain. You both taught me to give, always, as much as you have, and then some. תִּהְיֶינָה נַפְשׁוֹתֵיהֶם צְרוּרוֹת בִּצְרוֹר הַחַיִּים. Though it is hardly enough, I give this book to you.

About the Author

Tikva Hecht is a writer, editor, and educator. She earned her MFA in poetry from the University of California, Riverside and also holds an MA in philosophy from the New School for Social Research. She currently serves as the editorial director at Aleph Beta. *Tashlikh* is her first poetry collection.

The Jewish Poetry Project

jpoetry.us

Ben Yehuda Press

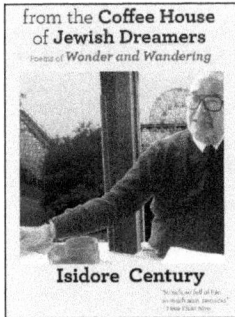

From the Coffee House of Jewish Dreamers: Poems of Wonder and Wandering and the Weekly Torah Portion by Isidore Century

"Isidore Century is a wonderful poet. His poems are funny, deeply observed, without pretension." —*The Jewish Week*

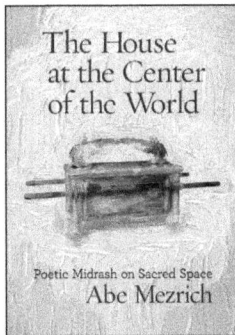

The House at the Center of the World: Poetic Midrash on Sacred Space by Abe Mezrich

"Direct and accessible, Mezrich's midrashic poems often tease profound meaning out of his chosen Torah texts. These poems remind us that our Creator is forgiving, that the spiritual and physical can inform one another, and that the supernatural can be carried into the everyday."
—Yehoshua November, author of *God's Optimism*

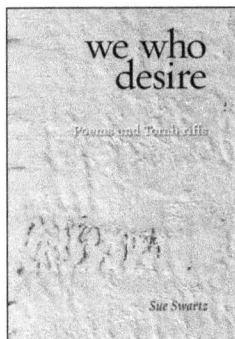

we who desire: Poems and Torah riffs by Sue Swartz

"Sue Swartz does magnificent acrobatics with the Torah. She takes the English that's become staid and boring, and adds something that's new and strange and exciting. These are poems that leave a taste in your mouth, and you walk away from them thinking, what did I just read? Oh, yeah. It's the Bible."
—Matthue Roth, author, *Yom Kippur A Go-Go*

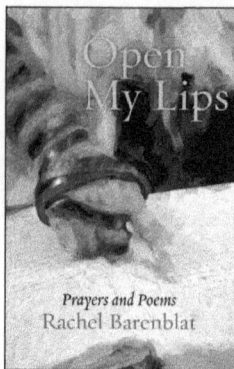

Open My Lips: Prayers and Poems
by Rachel Barenblat

"Barenblat's God is a personal God—one who lets her cry on His shoulder, and who rocks her like a colicky baby. These poems bridge the gap between the ineffable and the human. This collection will bring comfort to those with a religion of their own, as well as those seeking a relationship with some kind of higher power."
—Satya Robyn, author, *The Most Beautiful Thing*

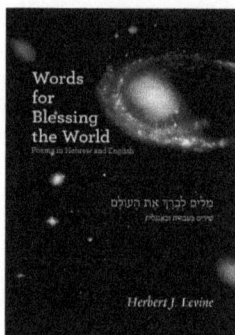

Words for Blessing the World: Poems in Hebrew and English by Herbert J. Levine

"These writings express a profoundly earth-based theology in a language that is clear and comprehensible. These are works to study and learn from."
—Rodger Kamenetz, author, *The Jew in the Lotus*

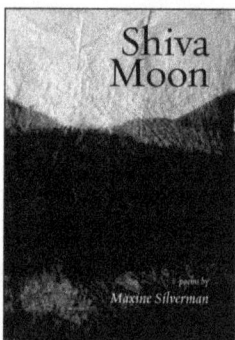

Shiva Moon: Poems by Maxine Silverman

"The poems, deeply felt, are spare, spoken in a quiet but compelling voice, as if we were listening in to her inner life. This book is a precious record of the transformation saying Kaddish can bring. It deserves to be read."
—Howard Schwartz, author, *The Library of Dreams*

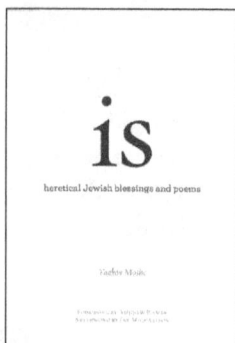

is: heretical Jewish blessings and poems
by Yaakov Moshe (Jay Michaelson)

"Finally, Torah that speaks to and through the lives we are actually living: expanding the tent of holiness to embrace what has been cast out, elevating what has been kept down, advancing what has been held back, reveling in questions, revealing contradictions."
—Eden Pearlstein, aka eprhyme

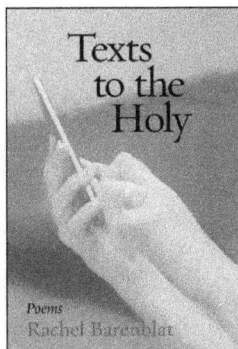

Texts to the Holy: Poems
by Rachel Barenblat

"These poems are remarkable, radiating a love of God that is full bodied, innocent, raw, pulsating, hot, drunk. I can hardly fathom their faith but am grateful for the vistas they open. I will sit with them, and invite you to do the same."
—Merle Feld, author of A Spiritual Life.

The Sabbath Bee: Love Songs to Shabbat
by Wilhelmina Gottschalk

"Torah, say our sages, has seventy faces. As these prose poems reveal, so too does Shabbat. Here we meet Shabbat as familiar housemate, as the child whose presence transforms a family, as a spreading tree, as an annoying friend who insists on being celebrated, as a woman, as a man, as a bee, as the ocean."
—Rachel Barenblat, author, *The Velveteen Rabbi's Haggadah*

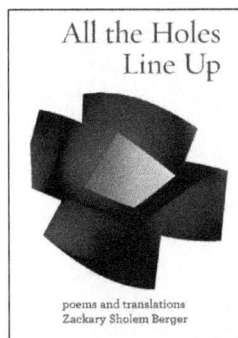

All the Holes Line Up: Poems and Translations
by Zackary Sholem Berger

"Spare and precise, Berger's poems gaze unflinchingly at—but also celebrate—human imperfection in its many forms. And what a delight that Berger also includes in this collection a handful of his resonant translations of some of the great Yiddish poets."
—Yehoshua November, author of *God's Optimism* and *Two World Exist*

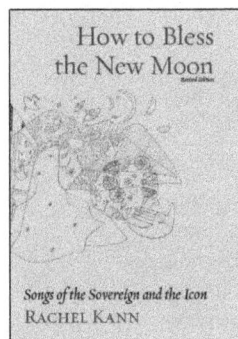

How to Bless the New Moon: Songs of the Sovereign and the Icon
by Rachel Kann

"Rachel Kann is a master wordsmith. Her poems are rich in content, packed with life's wisdom and imbued with soul. May this collection of her work enable more of the world to enjoy her offerings."
—Sarah Yehudit Schneider, author of *You Are What You Hate*

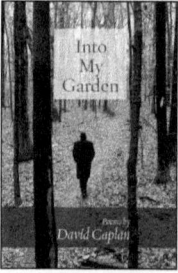

Into My Garden: Prayers
by David Caplan

"The beauty of Caplan's book is that it is not polemical. It does not set out to win an argument or ask you whether you've put your tefillin on today. These gentle poems invite the reader into one person's profound, ambiguous religious experience."
—*The Jewish Review of Books*

Between the Mountain and the Land is the Lesson:
Poetic Midrash on Sacred Community by Abe Mezrich

"Abe Mezrich cuts straight back to the roots of the Midrashic tradition, sermonizing as a poet, rather than ideologue. Best of all, Abe knows how to ask questions and avoid the obvious answers."
—Jake Marmer, author, *Jazz Talmud*

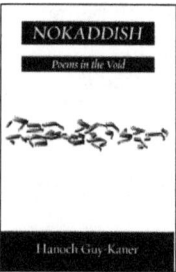

NOKADDISH: Poems in the Void
by Hanoch Guy Kaner

"A subversive, midrashic play with meanings—specifically Jewish meanings, and then the reversal and negation of these meanings."
—Robert G. Margolis

An Added Soul: Poems for a New Old Religion
by Herbert J. Levine

"Herbert J. Levine's lovely poems swing wide the double doors of English and Hebrew and open on the awe of being. Clear and direct, at ease in both tongues, these lyrics embrace a holiness unyoked from myth and theistic searching."
—Lynn Levin, author, *The Minor Virtues*

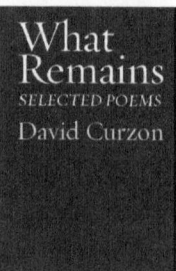

What Remains
by David Curzon

"Aphoristic, ekphrastic, and precise revelations animate WHAT REMAINS. In his stunning rewriting of Psalm 1 and other biblical passages, Curzon shows himself to be a fabricator, a collector, and an heir to the literature, arts, and wisdom traditions of the planet."
—Alicia Ostriker, author of *The Volcano and After*

The Shortest Skirt in Shul
by Sass Oron

"These poems exuberantly explore gender, Torah, the masks we wear, and the way our bodies (and the ways we wear them) at once threaten stable narratives, and offer the kind of liberation that saves our lives."
—Alicia Jo Rabins, author of *Divinity School*, composer of *Girls In Trouble*

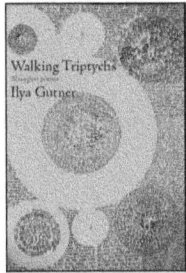

Walking Triptychs
by Ilya Gutner

These are poems from when I walked about Shanghai and thought about the meaning of the Holocaust.

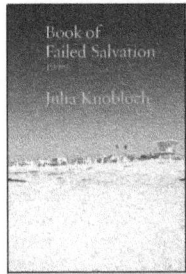

Book of Failed Salvation
by Julia Knobloch

"These beautiful poems express a tender longing for spiritual, physical, and emotional connection. They detail a life in movement—across distances, faith, love, and doubt."
—David Caplan, author, *Into My Garden*

Daily Blessings: Poems on Tractate Berakhot
by Hillel Broder

"Hillel Broder does not just write poetry about the Talmud; he also draws out the Talmud's poetry, finding lyricism amidst legality and re-setting the Talmud's rich images like precious gems in end-stopped lines of verse."
—Ilana Kurshan, author of *If All the Seas Were Ink*

The Red Door: A dark fairy tale told in poems
by Shawn C. Harris

"THE RED DOOR, like its poet author Shawn C. Harris, transcends genres and identities. It is an exploration in crossing worlds. It brings together poetry and story telling, imagery and life events, spirit and body, the real and the fantastic, Jewish past and Jewish present, to spin one tale." —Einat Wilf, author, *The War of Return*

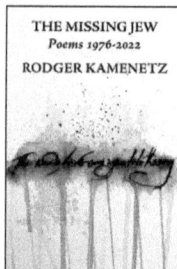

The Missing Jew: Poems 1976-2022
by Rodger Kamenetz

"How does Rodger Kamenetz manage to have so singular a voice and at the same time precisely encapsulate the world view of an entire generation (also mine) of text-hungry American Jews born in the middle of the twentieth century?"
—Jacqueline Osherow, author, *Ultimatum from Paradise* and *My Lookalike at the Krishna Temple: Poems*

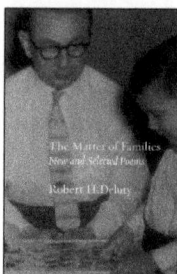

The Matter of Families
by Robert H. Deluty

"Robert Deluty's career-spanning collection of New and Selected poems captures the essence of his work: the power of love, joy, and connection, all tied together with the poet's glorious sense of humor. This book is Deluty's masterpiece."
—Richard M. Berlin, M.D., author of *Freud on My Couch*

There Is No Place Without You
by Maya Bernstein

"Bernstein's poems brim with energy and sound, moving the reader around a world mapped by motherhood, contemplation, religion, and the effects of illness on the body and spirit. Her language is lyrical, delicate, and poised; her lens is lucid and original."
—Anthony Anaxagorou, author of *After the Formalities*

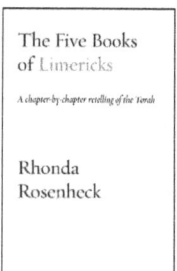

Torah Limericks
by Rhonda Rosenheck

"Rhonda Rosenheck knows the Hebrew Bible, and she knows that it can stand up to the sometimes silly, sometimes snarky, but always insightful scholarship packed into each one of these interpretive jewels."
—Rabbi Hillel Norry

Words for a Dazzling Firmament
by Abe Mezrich

"Mezrich is a cultivated craftsman: interpretively astute, sonically deliberate, and spiritually cunning."

—Zohar Atkins, author of *Nineveh*

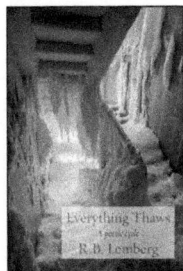

Everything Thaws
by R. B. Lemberg

"Full of glacier-sharp truths, and moments revealed between words like bodies beneath melting permafrost. As it becomes increasingly plain how deeply our world is shaped by war and climate change and grief and anger, articulating that shape feels urgent and necessary."
—Ruthanna Emrys, author of *A Half-Built Garden*

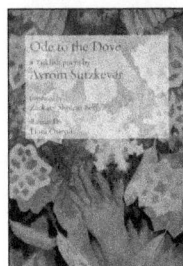

Ode to the Dove: *An illustrated, bilingual edition of a Yiddish poem by Abraham Sutzkever*
Zackary Sholem Berger, translator
Liora Ostroff, Illustrator

"An elegant volume for lovers of poetry."
—Justin Cammy, translator of *Sutzkever, From the Vilna Ghetto to Nuremberg: Memoir and Testimony*

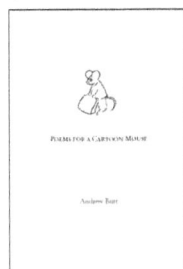

Poems for a Cartoon Mouse
by Andrew Burt

"Andrew Burt's poetry magnifies the vanishingly small line between danger and safety. This collection asks whether order is an illusion that veils chaos, or vice-versa, juxtaposing images from the Bible with animated films."
—Ari Shapiro, host of NPR's *All Things Considered*

Old Shul
by Pinny Bulman

"Nostalgia gives way to a tender theology, a softly chuckling illumination from within the heart of/as a beautiful, broken sanctuary, somehow both gritty and fragile, grimy and iridescent – not unlike faith itself."
—Jake Marmer, author of *Cosmic Diaspora*

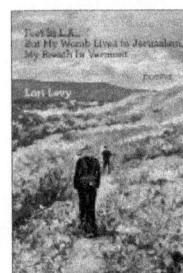

Feet In L.A., But My Womb Lives In Jerusalem, My Breath In Vermont
by Lori Levy

"Takes my breath away. With no pretense whatsoever, they leap, alive, from the page until this reader felt as if she were living Levy's life. How does the author do it?"
—Mary Jo Balistreri, author of *Still*

Bits and Pieces: A Roaming
by Edward Pomerantz

"A natural dramatist who looks back on his life growing up in Washington Heights in a series of vivid vignettes inspired by his early moviegoing."
—Robert Vas Dias, author of *Poetics Of Still Life: A Collage*

poem hashavua: A Personal Engagement with the Weekly Torah Portion in Poems and Pictures
by Lexie Botzum and Jessica Spencer, with full color illustrations by Arielle Stein and Claire Abramovitz
"Ancient and modern literary interpretations that carve out the negative space of the Torah's letters so that they dance before us as joyously as when they were given in fire on Sinai."
—Ilana Kurshan, author of *If All the Seas Were Ink*

So Many Warm Words: *Selections from the Poetry of Rosa Nevadovska - a bilingual edition*
translated by Merle L. Bachman

"Poems of loneliness and longing countered by others expressing joyous moments of transcendence... an opportunity to discover a poet whose verse offers moments of exquisite beauty."
—Sheva Zucker, editor emerita of *Afn Shvel.*

Styx by Else Lasker-Schüler
translated by Mildred Faintly

"Reborn in Mildred Faintly's magnificent translation, Else Lasker-Schüler's STYX overflows with shudders of desolation, moans of sexual pleasure, ecstatic fusions of love and despite that exalt and torture in equal measure."
—Joy Ladin, author *The Book of Anna* and *Shekhinah Speaks.*

Take a Breath, You're Getting Excited: *a bilingual edition of Hebrew poems* by Yakir Ben Moshe
translated by Dan Alter
"An unstoppable energy that only few contemporary poets, anywhere, possess... terrific use of tone, which is delivered in English that manages to be both clear and textured, memorably direct and yet intriguing."
—Ilya Kaminsky, author of *Deaf Republic* and *Dancing in Odessa*

www.ingramcontent.com/pod-product-compliance
Lightning Source LLC
LaVergne TN
LVHW041339080426
835512LV00006B/542